Glenda Jackson

The
Biography

By

Howard H. Curry

Table of Contents

Introduction

Glenda Jackson is a well-known politician and actor. She has accomplished significant work in both areas over a very long period of time. This biography provides a comprehensive look at Glenda Jackson's life and accomplishments, tracing her rise from accomplished actress to formidable political figure.

Glenda Jackson's upbringing and background, including her education and experiences that influenced her interest in the performing arts, will be revealed in this book. We will examine her breakthrough roles, the critical acclaim she received, and the numerous awards she received for her outstanding performances to trace her rise to prominence in the theater industry.

In addition, this biography examines Glenda Jackson's transition from stage to screen, focusing on her notable film roles and successful television ventures. In a similar vein, it sheds light on her astonishing and energizing shift into legislative issues, as well as her political activism and support, and the impact she has had in this field.

As we travel through Glenda Jackson's life, we will also gain insight into her own life, including her connections, family, and interests outside of her professional endeavors. We will examine her legacy, her later career, and the numerous accolades, awards, and accomplishments that shaped her illustrious path.

Chapter 1: Background and Early Life

Glenda Jackson was born in Birkenhead, Cheshire, England, on May 9, 1936. She came from a working-class family and was the youngest of four children. Her mother, Joan Jackson, was a cleaner, and her father, William Jackson, was a bricklayer. As a child growing up in a modest family, Glenda had to deal with the difficulties and difficulties that came with having limited financial resources.

Regardless of the requirements of her childhood, Glenda Jackson showed a sharp keenness and an energy for gaining since early on. She began to develop her intellectual abilities at West Kirby Grammar School for Girls. Glenda discovered her love for drama and the performing arts while she was in school.

During her time at RADA (Royal Academy of Dramatic Art), where she honed her skills and immersed herself in the theater world, her interest in acting grew even more. At RADA, she received comprehensive training that provided her with a solid foundation for her future acting career and a path to advancement.

Building a Career in Acting

Following her education at RADA, Glenda Jackson made her professional stage debut at the Liverpool Playhouse in 1957. She was offered more prominent roles in various theatrical productions as soon as she received recognition for her exceptional talent.

Glenda's career took off thanks to her dedication to her craft and her capacity to portray a wide range of characters with depth and authenticity. Her considerable stage presence, definitive voice, and astounding acting reach enraptured crowds and pundits the same.

Glenda worked a lot in regional theaters at the beginning of her career, gaining valuable experience and a solid reputation as a versatile and talented performer. By her dedication to her field and unwavering determination to succeed, she was on her way to much more prestigious opportunities and recognition in the years to come.

As her skills continued to shine, it became abundantly clear that Glenda Jackson's career was destined for higher positions. Her upbringing, education, and unwavering pursuit of excellence shaped her remarkable career as one of the most admired and acclaimed actresses of her time.

Chapter 2: Rise to Prominence

Glenda Jackson's exceptional talent and dedication to her craft may be to blame for her meteoric rise to stardom in the acting industry. In the 1960s, she started receiving a lot of attention for her powerful and memorable performances, which helped her establish a name for herself in the theater industry.

"The Persecution and Assassination of Jean-Paul Marat as Performed by the Inmates of the Asylum of Charenton under the Direction of the Marquis de Sade," also known as "Marat/Sade," was one of her notable early roles. She played Charlotte Corday in the play. Critics praised this performance because it showed her ability to bring complex characters to life.

Breakthrough Roles

Glenda Jackson played the eponymous character in the Royal Shakespeare Company's 1964 production of "Marat/Sade" at the Aldwych Theatre in London. This was her first substantial role. She became well-known as a result of her performance as Charlotte Corday and the success of the play.

Her stage roles as other well-known characters further demonstrated her exceptional talent and adaptability. When George Bernard Shaw's "Saint Joan" opened on Broadway in 1966, she gave a stunning performance as Saint Joan, which won her the first of two Tony Awards for Best Actress in a Play.

Glenda Jackson became well-known for her work in front of an audience and for collaborating with Harold Pinter, a well-known chief and dramatist.

Her performances in Pinter's plays, such as "The Homecoming" and "Old Times," demonstrated that she was able to deal with the complicated relationships between his characters and further established her reputation as a great actress.

Awards and Honors

Throughout her career, Glenda Jackson received numerous awards and honors for her exceptional talent and dedication to her craft. She won numerous prestigious awards for her stage performances, including the Laurence Olivier Award and numerous Evening Standard Theatre Awards, in addition to her Tony Awards.

Her exceptional achievements in front of an audience laid the basis for an effective profession in film and TV, further raising her remaining as a noticeable figure in media outlets. Glenda Jackson's rise to fame was not only due to her incredible talent but also to her unwavering dedication to her craft and her capacity to rivet audiences with her performances.

Chapter 3: Transition from Stage to Film and Television

Glenda Jackson's transition from Stage to Film and Television provided her with new opportunities to showcase her striking talent and connect with a broader audience. The seamless transfer of her captivating presence and versatility as an actress to the screen further solidified her formidable status as a performer.

She made her acting debut in the 1969 film adaptation of D.H.

Lawrence's novel "Women in Love," playing Gudrun Brangwen. Her fearless and nuanced performance in the film earned her international critical acclaim. For her role as Gudrun, Glenda Jackson won the Academy Award for Best Actress, establishing her as a formidable competitor in the film industry.

Notable Film Roles

Following her success in "Women in Love," Glenda Jackson continued to perform challenging roles of varying complexity in British and international films. She effortlessly switched genres and portrayed a variety of characters, demonstrating her adaptability.

One of her most notable film roles was playing Queen Elizabeth I in the historical drama "Mary, Queen of Scots" (1971), for which she was nominated for an additional Academy Award. Her performance, which was regal and authoritative, accurately conveyed the essence of the iconic queen and further established her reputation as an adaptable actress who is capable of portraying complex historical figures.

Glenda Jackson demonstrated her versatility in both contemporary films and historical dramas. She gave strong performances in films like "Sunday Bloody Sunday" (1971), "A Touch of Class" (1973), and "Hedda" (1975) that demonstrated her ability to give characters who were complex and had strong emotions depth and authenticity.

Achievements in Television

Glenda Jackson's talent and presence transcended the screen. In addition, she made memorable appearances on television in roles that further showcased her versatility and acting abilities.

Her portrayal of Elizabeth I in the BBC miniseries "Elizabeth R" in 1971 was one of her most well-known roles on television. She won two Emmy Awards for Outstanding Lead Entertainer in a Show Series and a BAFTA Television Award for her performance as the notorious monarch.

With her move into film and television, Glenda Jackson was able to connect with audiences all over the world. She was one of the most talented and well-liked actresses of her generation thanks to her outstanding performances on both big and small screens. She also had a lasting impact on the film and television industries.

Chapter 4: Politics as a career

Glenda Jackson entered politics in an unexpected and bold move to begin a new chapter in her life. She made the decision to enter politics in order to combine her highly successful acting career with her passion for social justice and public service.

After joining the British Labour Party in 1992, Glenda Jackson became an MP for the London constituency of Hampstead and Highgate. Her desire to advocate for the rights and well-being of her constituents and have a measurable impact on the issues she was deeply concerned about was the driving force behind her decision to enter politics.

Political Activism and Advocacy

Throughout her political career, Glenda Jackson demonstrated a determined commitment to social causes and a fierce devotion to her constituents. She became well-known for her ardent support of education, healthcare, housing, and women's rights.

While Glenda Jackson was an MP, she actively participated in parliamentary debates and fought for policies that aimed to address societal inequalities and promote fairness and justice. She was a vocal advocate for affordable housing, frequently raising concerns about the housing crisis and looking for solutions to ensure that everyone had sufficient housing.

Glenda Jackson was also an advocate for women's rights and gender equality. She actively supported policies and legislation in the areas of combating gender-based violence, reproductive rights, and workplace gender equality.

Impact and Achievements

Glenda Jackson's political career was marked by her unwavering devotion to her constituents and the causes she believed in. Her advocacy and legislative work had a lasting impact on the communities she served, and she was a major influence on significant policy changes.

She worked to make housing more affordable and accessible to individuals and families and had a significant impact on housing policy. Her unwavering efforts in this area helped to raise awareness of the housing crisis and prompted significant changes to the way the problem is dealt with.

In addition, Glenda Jackson was a supporter of undervalued networks and the power of involving one's foundation to effect change. Her capacity to use her position to amplify the voices of the underrepresented and her unwavering commitment to social justice demonstrated her unwavering determination to have a positive impact on society.

Despite the fact that Glenda Jackson's political career came to an end in 2015 when she decided not to run for president, her legacy as a zealous advocate and champion of social causes continues to inspire others to get involved in politics and work toward a society that is more equitable and fair.

Chapter 5: Personal Life

Glenda Jackson has kept her personal relationships private and remained committed to her career in her personal life. She has focused heavily on her professional endeavors while keeping her personal life out of the public eye.

Jackson was married to fellow actor Roy Hodges from 1958 to 1976. The couple's son Dan Hodges went on to become a political commentator and journalist.

Despite the lack of information regarding her romantic relationships since her divorce, Glenda Jackson has emphasized the importance of maintaining a balance between her professional and personal lives. She has made the decision to keep her intimate relationships out of the public eye so that she can keep her privacy when it comes to them.

Hobbies and Interests

Glenda Jackson has a wide range of interests and pursuits outside of her successful acting and political career. She has communicated an adoration for writing and is known to be an eager peruser, notwithstanding her bustling timetable. Her deep understanding of the characters she portrays and her love of reading have both had an impact on her performances.

Glenda Jackson is well-known for her love of literature and her interest in art and painting. She has discovered her creative side through painting, which is an outlet for both solace and self-expression.

Additionally, Glenda Jackson has advocated for environmentalists. She has demonstrated a commitment to raising awareness of sustainability and climate change by using her platform to emphasize the significance of preserving the environment for future generations.

Glenda Jackson has demonstrated a multifaceted personality in addition to her professional accomplishments by pursuing personal interests and participating in causes that are dear to her. Her capacity to strike a balance and cultivate her passions outside of her work contributes to her overall contentment and well-roundedness as a person.

Chapter 6: Later Career and Legacy

Glenda Jackson returned to the stage in 2016 after taking a break from acting to concentrate on her political career. At the Old Vic Theatre in London, she made her comeback in the title role of William Shakespeare's "King Lear." She received a lot of praise for her performance as the complex and tragic monarch because it brought to mind her exceptional talent and commanding stage presence.

Glenda Jackson has continued to captivate audiences with nuanced performances in challenging and iconic roles ever since her return. Her later work stands out for its depth and authenticity in its portrayal of a wide range of characters. She has become a true icon of the performing arts by consistently demonstrating her remarkable range as an actress, whether on stage or screen.

Remarkable Performances

Late in Career In notable productions in recent years, Glenda Jackson has given strong performances. She was praised by critics for her performance as Aline Solness in "The Master Builder" by Henrik Ibsen at the Old Vic Theatre in 2019, demonstrating her subtlety and depth in navigating Ibsen's complex characters.

She appeared in Friedrich Dürrenmatt's "The Visit" at the National Theatre in London in 2020 as the well-known title character. In her compelling performance, Claire Zachanassian demonstrated her mastery of roles that are both complex and morally ambiguous. She played a wealthy woman in a small town who is on the lookout for vengeance.

Influence and Contributions to the Industry

Glenda Jackson's decades-long contributions to the performing arts industry have left a lasting impression on the stage and film. Generations of actors and actresses have looked up to her as an example of excellence in the acting industry because of her talent, versatility, and dedication to her craft.

Glenda Jackson is remembered for her groundbreaking political career in addition to her outstanding performances. Her decision to support social causes and use her platform and influence to serve the public demonstrated her unwavering commitment to enhancing society.

Her ability to seamlessly switch between politics and acting demonstrates Glenda Jackson's versatility and determination to use her voice for real change. People who want to combine their talents with a commitment to social justice should be inspired by her influence on the political and performing arts industries.

Glenda Jackson is still celebrated and appreciated by audiences, fellow actors, and activists alike for her contributions as a respected figure. Her legacy as a true entertainment icon and a champion of causes that resonate with the human experience has been solidified by her influence as an actress and her unwavering commitment to making a difference.

Chapter 7: Awards and Honors

Throughout her long career, Glenda Jackson has been recognized for her exceptional talent and contributions to the arts with numerous awards and honors. She has received praise from critics and recognition from prestigious institutions in the entertainment industry for her outstanding stage and screen performances.

Her notable accomplishments include the following:

Oscars for "Women in Love" in 1971 for Best Actress Glenda Jackson's performance as Gudrun Brangwen established her as a leading actress in the industry.

Tony Awards for her performance in "Strange Interlude" as Best Actress: For her performance as Nina Leeds in Eugene O'Neill's play, Glenda Jackson won a Tony Award, showcasing her incredible talent on Broadway.

For "Marat/Sade" in 1966, she won the award for Best Actress in a Play. She won a Tony Award for her performance as Charlotte Corday in the Royal Shakespeare

Company production, demonstrating her capacity to captivate audiences.

Emmy Awards for Extraordinary Lead Entertainer in a Show Series for "Elizabeth R," 1972: Glenda Jackson won two Emmy Awards for her role as Queen Elizabeth I in the BBC miniseries, demonstrating her remarkable ability on the small screen.

BAFTA Awards for Best Actress for "Women in Love" (1971) and "Sunday Bloody Sunday" (1972): For her outstanding roles in these films, Glenda Jackson received two BAFTA Awards, confirming her status as an accomplished and versatile actress.

Honors and Awards for the Evening Standard Theater: Throughout her career, Glenda Jackson has won numerous Evening Standard Theatre Awards for her outstanding stage performances.

Award for Laurence Olivier: She has also been recognized for her contributions to the British theater scene with the prestigious Laurence Olivier Award.

Honorary admission to the American Theater Hall of Fame:

Glenda Jackson was included in the American Theater Lobby of Notoriety to honor her notable career and dedication to the theater. As a result, her reputation as an outstanding actress grew even stronger.

Glenda Jackson's extraordinary talent, versatility, and impact on the acting industry are demonstrated by these awards. Her accomplishments are evidence of her lasting legacy in the entertainment industry, and her work continues to receive praise.

Chapter 8: Beyond her outstanding performances

Glenda Jackson has had a significant impact on society and the arts. She has consistently pushed boundaries and used her platform to advocate for social change throughout her career. She has made numerous contributions to society and the arts:

Empowerment and Representation

Glenda Jackson's status as a powerful and successful actress has had a significant impact on how women working in the entertainment industry are portrayed. She broke barriers and paved the way for future generations of actresses by being a woman in a field that was mostly dominated by men. Women who are interested in careers in acting and other creative fields have found strength and inspiration in her resilience and success.

Advocacy for the Disadvantaged and Social Justice

Glenda Jackson's political career and artistic work demonstrated her commitment to social justice and advocacy. She actively advocated for housing, healthcare, education, and women's rights as a Member of Parliament. Numerous lives have been improved as a result of her advocacy for these causes and for those whose voices are frequently silenced.

Influence on Acting and Execution

Glenda Jackson had a profound influence on acting. She has become a role model for other performers around the world thanks to her extraordinary talent, adaptability, and dedication to her craft. Many actors and actresses have been inspired to push the boundaries of their own artistic expression by her ability to authentically and deeply portray a variety of complex characters.

Opening Dialogues and Challenges to Conventions

Over the course of her career, Glenda Jackson has been involved in a variety of roles and projects that provoke thought, challenge conventions, and address significant social issues. She has chosen roles that focus on societal inequality and the complexities of human nature. This has sparked meaningful discussions and prompted audiences to consider pressing social and political issues.

Inspirational Legacy

Glenda Jackson's influence on art and society extends beyond her own generation. Her standing for boldness, expertise, and advancement keeps on rousing both current and future Craftsman's to involve their establishment for positive change. We are constantly reminded of the transformative power of storytelling and the arts because of her contributions, which have shaped our collective consciousness.

Glenda Jackson's remarkable talent, unwavering commitment to social justice, and extensive body of work demonstrate her influence on art and society. Her legacy inspires activists, artists, and everyone in between to strive for excellence, question conventional wisdom, and make a big difference in the world.

The life and work of Glenda Jackson demonstrate the power of talent, perseverance, and unwavering dedication to one's profession and beliefs. She has captivated audiences with her exceptional performances and left an indelible mark on the acting industry, from her early days in the theater to her triumphant return to the stage and screen.

Glenda Jackson's political career demonstrated her enthusiasm for social justice and determination to positively influence society in addition to her artistic accomplishments. Her legacy as a champion for others' rights and welfare was further consolidated by her advocacy and work as a Member of Parliament.

Even after she has left the spotlight, Glenda Jackson has had an impact on art and society. She has broken down barriers and used her platform to speak up for the underrepresented and open doors for future generations. Actors, artists, and others who wish to effect real change can draw inspiration from her legacy.

We are reminded of the transformative power of storytelling, the significance of using one's voice for social justice, and the limitless potential of the human spirit as we reflect on Glenda Jackson's remarkable journey. Her legacy will continue to influence acting, politics, and other fields for many years to come.

Due to her unwavering dedication, exceptional talent, and determination to make a difference, Glenda Jackson has left a lasting impression on society, art, and the hearts of many admirers. Her legacy will continue to have an impact because it will serve as a reminder of the significant impact that one person can have when they courageously pursue their passions and defend their beliefs.

Conclusion

In conclusion, the life and work of Glenda Jackson demonstrate a remarkable individual's accomplishments and influence. She rose to prominence as a political and acting pioneer from humble beginnings. She rose to prominence in her field thanks to her exceptional talent, adaptability, and dedication, which earned her numerous accolades. Jackson's political career demonstrated her unwavering commitment to equality and social justice beyond her artistic endeavors. Artists and activists of all ages have been inspired by her legacy to use their platforms to effect positive change. The extraordinary journey of Glenda Jackson is a shining example of how talent, enthusiasm, and perseverance can change everything.

Printed in Great Britain
by Amazon

33749985R00036